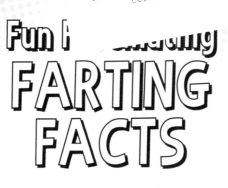

Fun Facts
FARTING
FACTS

Plus a feast of funny, finger-pulling
fart jokes to blow off the blues!

Concept by Jamien Bailey

B3

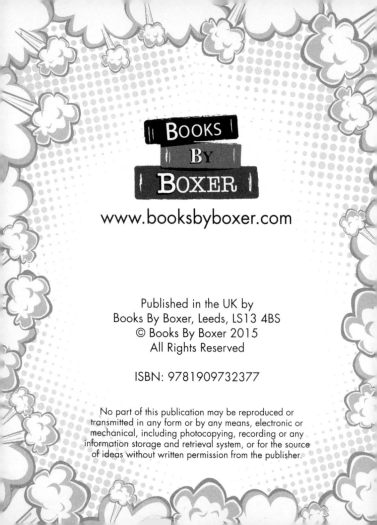

BOOKS BY BOXER

www.booksbyboxer.com

Published in the UK by
Books By Boxer, Leeds, LS13 4BS
© Books By Boxer 2015
All Rights Reserved

ISBN: 9781909732377

These cherished thoughts are good for your heart. The more you read, the more you'll fart!

1.

The typical fart is composed of about 59% nitrogen, 21% hydrogen, 9% carbon dioxide, 7% methane and 4% oxygen – all odourless gases. Less than one percent of a fart contains hydrogen sulphide gas, ammonia and excrement. The sulphur is what makes farts stink, and this can be smelled a 1 part per 100 million parts air.

2.

The more sulphur-rich your diet, the worse your farts will smell. Foods such as beans, cabbage, cheese and eggs contain higher levels of sulphur, which is why they cause farts so noxious they'll peel the paint off your walls!

PARPPP!

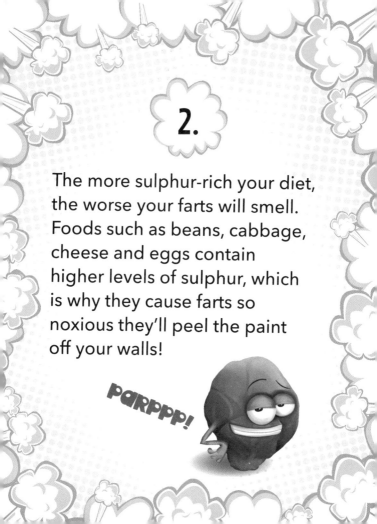

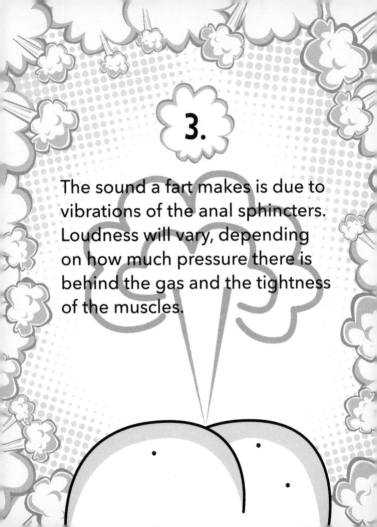

3.

The sound a fart makes is due to vibrations of the anal sphincters. Loudness will vary, depending on how much pressure there is behind the gas and the tightness of the muscles.

4.

The average person produces around 600ml of farts every day and, even though many women don't admit to trumping, they let rip just as often as men. In fact, it's been proven that when men and women eat exactly same food, women tend to have more concentrated levels of sulphur than men.

5.

Farts may be expelled with varying velocities, but you won't smell one until around 10-15 seconds after letting it go. This is how long it takes for the odorous gas to travel the room and reach your nostrils.

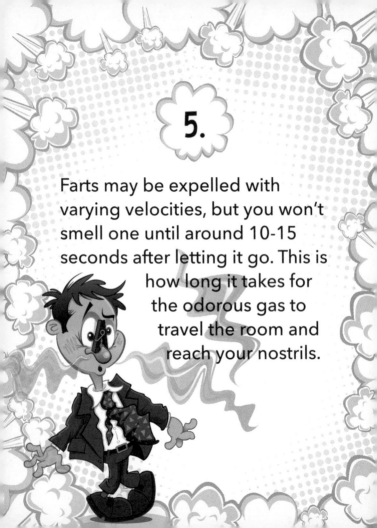

6.

Scientists disagree on whether holding in a fart is bad for the health. Some believe that wind is a simply a part of your digestive system and holding it in is harmless. Others say that, at best, keeping it in can cause uncomfortable bloating and, at worst, haemorrhoids or a distended bowel.

7.

Most cultures believe that farting should be stifled in polite company, but there are some cultures that actively enjoy social parps! The Yanomami, a tribe in South America, fart to greet one another, whilst in China you can get a job as a professional fart-smeller!

8.

An ancient Roman author reported that Emperor Claudius, fearing that holding farts in was bad for the health, passed an edict stating that it was acceptable to break wind – quietly or noisily – at the banqueting table.

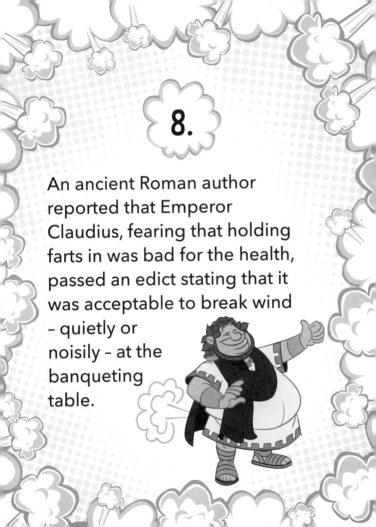

9.

The methane and hydrogen produced in farts can make them highly flammable. Holding a lighter to your bum and letting one go can be hilarious; producing a burst of flame, but it's clearly very dangerous and not recommended.

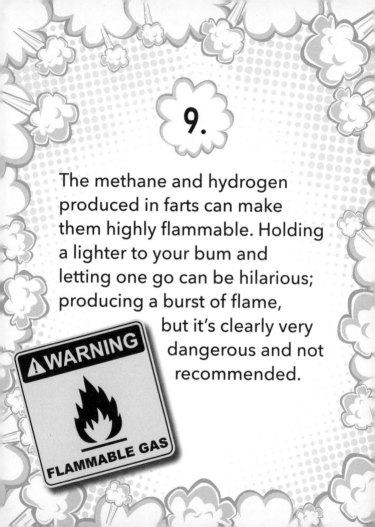

⚠WARNING

FLAMMABLE GAS

10.

Termites fart more than any other animal, making them the second largest natural source of methane emissions (cow burps are the first). Termites need high levels of methane-producing gut bacteria to digest all the wood they eat although the amount generated varies between different species.

11.

Even if you hold them in, farts will pop out when you sleep. The anal sphincter muscles relax when you're asleep, so they'll slip out without you noticing. You won't be awoken by the pong either, as sense of smell is reduced when sleeping.

paarrppp!!!

zzzZ

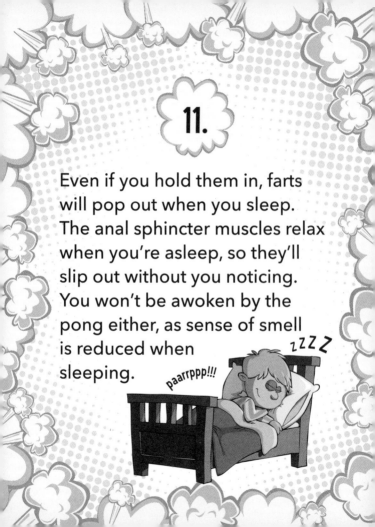

12.

Even once you've kicked the bucket, you'll carry on farting. Gases continue to be released from both ends of the digestive tract for up to three hours after death, resulting in burping or farting noises.

13.

Many people around the world enjoy chewing gum for the refreshing taste or to control bad breath. Some even use it as a study aid. But what they don't realise is that when gum is chewed, more air is swallowed. This can lead to increased (minty-fresh…?) flatulence.

14.

Another factor comes into play when chewing sugar-free gum, as well as consuming other sugar-free food and drinks. Most of them contain sweeteners like sorbitol or xylitol – which are known to cause excess gas and bad farts.

15.

An average, healthy human farts around 14-15 times a day. Don't believe what women say – they fart just as often as men.

16.

The word 'Fart' is one of the oldest in the English language. It originates from the middle English word feortan, in turn from the old High German ferzan, meaning 'break wind'.

17.

Don't believe anyone who tells you that they don't fart. Every living creature with a gut emits gas from their ass every single day.

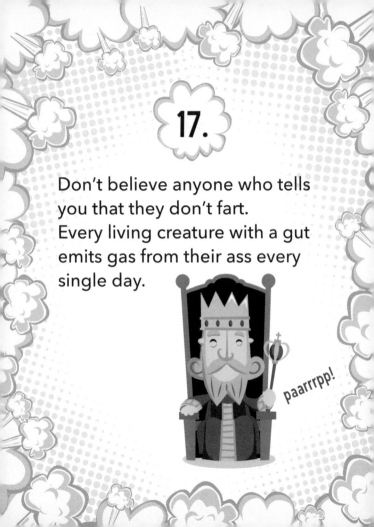

paarrrpp!

18.

A gentleman farts mostly in the bathroom. This is an excellent place to fart, providing good acoustics that can resonate wonderfully throughout the whole house, allowing everyone the opportunity to appreciate the depth and range of the sound.

19.

Beans contain sugars that we can't easily digest. This is why vegetarians tend to fart much more than those with a less limiting diet.

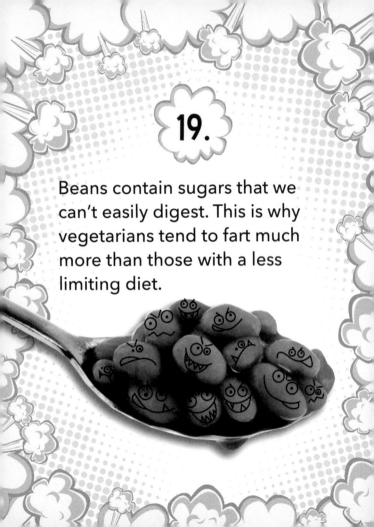

20.

Disappearing farts:
When farts disappear, they don't just evaporate! They go back to the place from whence they came, farther up the colon. Here, they lay dormant until you relax or fall asleep. Then they come back – with a vengeance!

FART!

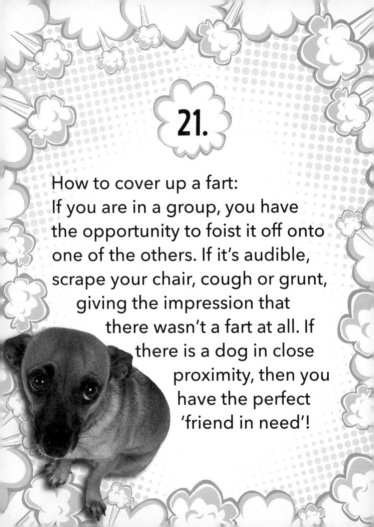

21.

How to cover up a fart:
If you are in a group, you have
the opportunity to foist it off onto
one of the others. If it's audible,
scrape your chair, cough or grunt,
giving the impression that
there wasn't a fart at all. If
there is a dog in close
proximity, then you
have the perfect
'friend in need'!

22.

Le Pétomane was a French flatulist (professional farter) and entertainer. He found fame by being able to seemingly fart at will. He debuted his speciality performance, which included such ripping tunes as 'a walk in the farmyard' and a rough rendering of O Sole Mio, in Marseilles in 1897.

23.

In 1892, Le Pétomane took his act to the Moulin Rouge in Paris. The initial attempt was met with some scepticism, but he quickly won the audience over and was a big success performing for King Leopold II and Sigmund Freud. It's said he could even use his bum to blow out a candle located several feet away.

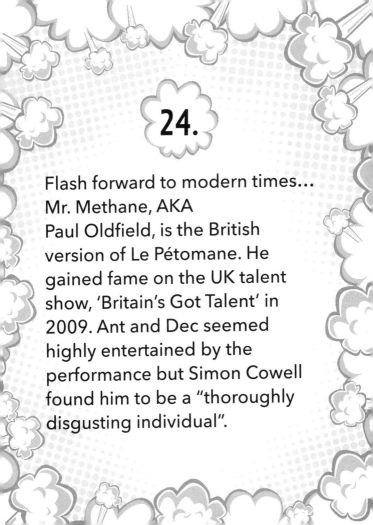

24.

Flash forward to modern times...
Mr. Methane, AKA
Paul Oldfield, is the British
version of Le Pétomane. He
gained fame on the UK talent
show, 'Britain's Got Talent' in
2009. Ant and Dec seemed
highly entertained by the
performance but Simon Cowell
found him to be a "thoroughly
disgusting individual".

25.

Fartiste, *noun*
An cultured individual who has completely mastered the art of the fart.

26.

The Whoopee Cushion, in its familiar rubber form, originated in Canada in the 1920s and became a best-seller for one Johnson Smith Company. It's still popular and the original design, featuring a shocked lady sitting on it with the slogan 'emits a real Bronx cheer', can still be bought today.

27.

He Gassen, or The Fart Battle is a series of Japanese scroll about farting. Dating from 300-400 years ago, the scrolls show men and women farting so fiercely that they knock people from horses and flatten them to the floor, blow holes in doors and buildings, fell trees and send cats and dogs flying into the air.

28.

Cupcake, *verb*
The amusing act of farting into one's hands before putting them over someone's face, so that they must inhale your gas.

29.

"Fart noises are hilarious, especially when made with one's armpits."

(Anonymous, although often credited to Mark Twain)

30.

Delivering a fart:
The best method, when sitting, is to lean over onto one leg and trump loudly into the cushions. If standing, then one must orient the rump in an opportune direction and let out a manly staccato blast. High-pitched or 'girly' farts are strictly to be avoided and are much frowned upon.

Once you have let rip, depending

on the location and general company, you should raise one's eyebrows as if totally surprised by the interjection, and then waft the hand to help others to gauge the likely stinky-ness of the imminent odour.

Following a fart with the saying 'better out than in' has these days fallen out of favour, as has the more schoolboy-like cry of 'get a load of that one'. The modern man will supply a jolly 'Wooahh!' if the delivery is impressive in volume or length. The follow-up fart, if one is brewing, can then be exclaimed with 'Good arse!' as an encouragement to one's bowels.

Remarking too quickly on a fellow's fart can be a dangerous affair. Calling out too quickly risks an accusation of 'first who smelt it, dealt it', a claim that must be followed by the retort 'the one who said the rhyme did the crime'. If there is a silent party present, the accused can declare 'the one who denied it supplied it'.

31.

For those at school, it is the acknowledged custom that, if one is near a kid who has just 'blown off' (or 'boffed'), one should loudly make an exclamation before burying one's nose beneath outer garments. Great care must be taken if near an individual who is bigger than oneself, as a good thumping will often be meted out to the emitter of the fart.

32.

The dog is a man's best friend and, of course, has a fondness for farts. When a dog's owner farts, the dog will get up - even from a nap - for a sniff of the crotch.

Dogs fart themselves, and those releases are usually silent and pretty deadly. Dog farts have been known to set off smoke alarms and carbon monoxide detectors, rendering these devices useless in many homes.

Having a dog is useful for a person whose farts are smelly because, after dropping a stink bomb, you can blame it on the dog who will happily take the credit.

Warning: cats do not fart and will attack any dog that farts near them. Probably any human, too.

33.

According to Uncyclopedia, the loudest fart ever recorded "occurred on 16 May 1972 in Madeline, Texas by Alvin Meshits. The blast maintained a level of 194 decibels for one third of a second. Mr. Meshits now has recurring back pain as a result of this feat." Delightful but, sadly, untrue.

34.

High levels of methane gas from 90 dairy cows built up inside a shed on a farm in the central German town of Rasdorf in January 2014 before, according to local police reports, "a static electric charge caused the gas to explode with flashes of flames". One cow was treated for burns, a police spokesman added.

35.

Dutch oven, *noun*
A term used to describe the act of pulling the bed covers over a partner's head whilst letting out a loud and smelly fart.

36.

Pyroflatulence, *verb*
The art of lighting one's farts
without setting fire to one's arse.
Also known as flatus ignition.
A successful fart lighter can
officially join the blue flame club.

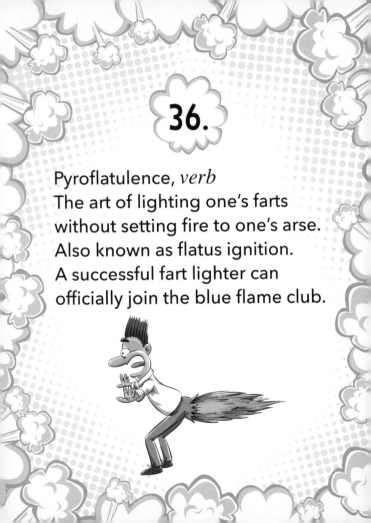

37.

US Marines in Afghanistan ordered not to fart: Audible farting was banned for some Marines because it could offend the cultural sensitivities of the Afghans. A Marine spokesperson stated, "We know not to talk about religion, politics or girls but farting is practically a sport around here!"

38.

The Flatulence Appreciation (Ripping & Trumping) Society (F.A.R.T.S.) awarded the following scenes with 'Top Trumps' – best fart scenes in a motion picture.

Blazing Saddles – Camp Fire Scene

Dumb and Dumber – Harry in the Bathroom/Lloyd Lights a Fire Fart

The Hollywood Knights – New Bomb Turk Sings 'Volare'

39.

The F.A.R.T.S 'SBD' (Silent But Deadly) runners up are:

Harold and Kumar Go to White Castle – Battle Shits

Click – Sandler Farts on Hasselhoff

The Nutty Professor – Dinner at the Klumps

40.

And, finally, their 'Wet Ones'

Naked Gun – Microphoned Bathroom Break

Scary Movie 4 – Blind Girl in the Wrong House

Shrek – Shrek farts taking a mud bath

41.

Actress Whoopi Goldberg was heard on US daytime TV programme, The View releasing an impressively loud fart. Commentators said this was louder than anything a Whoopee Cushion could make!

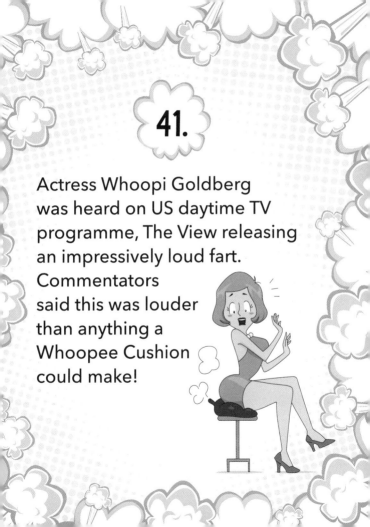

42.

Farts really can be deadly: In his book 'The Jewish War,' Roman author Josephus (37-100) describes an anti-Semitic Roman soldier who farted in front of a crowd of Jews as they celebrated Passover. According to the book, the soldier "pulled back his garment, and cowering down after an indecent manner, turned his breech to the Jews, and spake such words as you might expect upon such a posture."

The Jews were angered by this and began stoning the soldiers. The Roman leader of Jerusalem, Cumanus (it was his name, honest!), called in more soldiers and a riot took place. Most of the 10,000 people who were killed in the fray were Jews who trampled each other trying to escape when the Roman Army arrived.

43.

Hitler suffered from uncontrollable flatulence and was prescribed a cocktail of medication by his physician Dr Morrell. The drugs included up to 150 of Dr Koester's anti-gas pills a week, which contained strychnine. Although not lethal in tiny doses, it may have contributed in some way to the onset of madness.

44.

In New Zealand a 50 cent stamp was minted entitled, 'Sparrow Fart'. This is a slang term meaning 'the earliest part of the morning' (when sparrows wake and let out a little fart).

45.

According to IMDB, British actress Helena Bonham Carter eased the tension during a sex scene with co-star Paul Bettany on the set of the film Heart of Me by farting.

46.

In January 2003, museum officials at the Dewa Roman Experience in Chester, England, were forced to tone down the 2,000 year old smell of a Roman latrine when it made several visiting school kids throw up.

The man-made stink, called Flatulence, was created by Dale Air (www.daleair.com), an aroma manufacturing company in

Lancashire, England. "The smell was disgusting. It was like very strong boiled cabbage, sweet and sickly," the supervisors said.

47.

Two rare snakes from the American southwest – the deadly Sonoran Coral snake and the Western Hook-Nosed snake – both make farting noises to scare off predators. When threatened, they produce air bubbles from the cloaca, the opening for sex and excretion at a snake's rear end. The snake uses two sets of muscles to isolate a compressed pocket of air, which it then releases to the outside in a startling, explosive burst.

48.

Every year, San Jose University in California sponsors the Bulwer-Litton Fiction Contest, in which contestants attempt to write the most outrageous opening sentences for novels. In 1997, one of the runner-up entries was: 'As a scientist, Throckmorton knew that if he were ever to break wind in the sound chamber he would never hear the end of it'.

49.

One of the funniest TV show fart scenes is in Sex and the City, when Carrie accidentally farts whilst in bed with Big. She is so embarrassed that she decides to ignore the whole thing. In the evening, during a take away Chinese meal at home, Big slips a Whoopee Cushion on her chair as she momentarily rises. The resultant fart sound is outrageous, but outrageously funny!

50.

How long do you refrain from farting when you start dating someone new?

The answer, based on a survey conducted at UCLA (University of California) is generally about 1 month for the man and 2-3 months for a woman.

51.

In Herodotus' Histories, an Egyptian rebel leader named Amasis is said to have responded to a courier's request to meet with King Apries by raising his leg and farting, telling the messenger to take that back to his leader.

52.

When the Great Plague of London struck in 1665, plague doctors are believed to have created a very unusual cure; the fart jar.

To fight the symptoms of plague, people would fart into a jar and then deeply inhale the contents. Yes, people were sniffing their own trumps in an attempt to cure the plague.

The theory was, if bad smells caused plague, then the bad smells from a fart jar should fight off the plague-riddled air.

53.

Martin Luther, one of the founders of the Protestant church, was particularly fart-obsessed. He reportedly claimed to have once dismissed the Devil "mit einen Furz" ('with a fart') when the Satanic Lord paid a him courtesy call.

54.

In the animal world, hippos fart the loudest and longest, wagging their tails furiously as they do it. Hilarious.

55.

Never read any Geoffrey Chaucer?
This, then, from The Miller's Tale:
"This Nicholas anon leet fle a fart,
As greet as it had been a
thonder-dent,
That with the strook he was
almost yblent;
And he was redy with his
iren hoot,
And Nicholas amydde the ers
he smoot,

Of gooth the skyn an hande
brede aboute,
The hoote kultour brende so
his toute,

(Ye olde farting humour, what!)

And for the smert he wende for
to dye.
As he were wood, for wo he gan
to crye,
"Help! Water! Water! Help for
Goddes herte!"

Here are some hilariously farty jokes for you! Just be careful you don't let one drop because you're laughing so hard!

Why don't you fart in church?

Because you have to
sit in your pew!

The teacher asked little Billy to use the word "definitely" in a sentence. Little Billy replies, "Teacher, do farts have lumps in them?" The Teacher says, "Of course not Billy!" To which Billy replies, "Then I have definitely pooped my pants."

An elderly couple are at church one Sunday morning. Halfway through the service, the wife leans over and whispers in her husband's ear, "I've just let out a silent fart. What do you think I should do?" The husband replies, "Put a new battery in your hearing aid!"

Farts are like children...
you don't mind your own,
but can't stand anyone else's!

If you were to fart whilst travelling at the speed of sound, would you smell it before you heard it?

I silently farted in bed last night and slowly lifted up the quilt. After a few seconds my wife said "Good grief Brian, that stinks!" It must've been pretty awful, she was downstairs at the time!

I'm not saying my wife
has a loud fart...

but she'll never be
hit by a ship.

Why do farts smell?

So deaf people can
enjoy them too.

Is someone who farts
creatively a 'fartist'?

What happened when the
dinosaurs couldn't fart anymore?

They faced ex-stink-tion!

How can you tell if a
woman is wearing tights?

When she farts,
her ankles swell!

What's invisible and
smells of carrots?

The Easter Bunny's farts!

"Darling," says a husband coyly to his wife, "let's try different positions tonight."
"What a good idea," she replies. "You stand in front of the sink and do the dishes, and I'll sit in front of the TV and fart."

An old man's children had put him in the best rest home that money could buy. He even had a pair of orderlies who were by his side 24 hours a day. The children came to visit him and noticed that the old man would lean to the left and the orderly on that side would straighten him up. When he leaned to the right, that orderly straightened him up.

This went on throughout their visit. In the course of the conversation, his son asked him how he liked the home. "The home is fine" said Dad, "but it's this pair that give me trouble". "How come?" asked the son. "How come?? Every time I lean over to let out a fart, they won't let me!"

One evening, a very attractive young lady was sitting in a fine restaurant, waiting for her date to arrive. While waiting, she decided to make sure she looked perfect for him. So the young lady bent down in her chair to get a mirror from her handbag. Then, just as the waiter walked up, she accidentally farted quite loudly. The lady immediately sat up straight, embarrassed and red-faced, sure that everyone in the place had heard her. Quickly, she turned to the waiter to try and deflect the blame from her and says loudly, "Stop that!"

The waiter looked at her and replied dryly, "Of course madam. Which way was it headed?"

An elderly lady visits the doctor about a rather embarrassing problem. "Doctor, I can't stop passing wind. Luckily, my farts don't smell and are always silent. At home, when I'm with friends, at church, as a matter of fact, I've had three while sitting here talking to you. What can you do to help?" she asks.

The doctor replies, "The first thing we're going to do is check your hearing!"

What is green and smelly?

The Hulk's farts!

Two businessmen, one American and one Japanese, are out playing a round of golf. The Japanese man is getting ready to tee off and suddenly starts talking to his thumb.

The American man asks what he is doing?

"We develop micro-technology, I have a microphone in my thumb and I was just recording a message."

The two men carry on with their round of golf, when all of a sudden the American man makes a funny sound, suspiciously like a fart! The Japanese man looks at him accusingly...

"Oh," says the American, "don't worry, I'm just receiving a fax."

While at a dinner party, a man farts. Another guest is outraged and says "How dare you fart in front of my wife!"

"I'm so sorry," the first man says. "I didn't realise it was her turn."

A belch is but a gust of wind,
That cometh from the heart.
But should it take a downward turn,
It turneth to a fart!

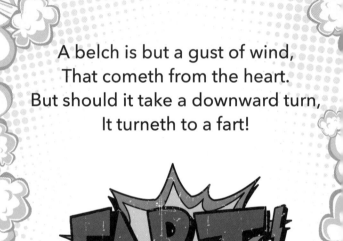